faux fabulous

Florals

four
seasons
of
easy
ideas

By **Colleen Mullaney**

sixth&spring
books

New York

Editorial Director
Trisha Malcolm

Art Director
Christy Hale

Cover Design
Chi Ling Moy

Copy Editor
Apollinaire Scherr
Pat Harste

Stylist
Laura Maffeo

Photographer
Jack Deutsch

Principal Photography Assistant
Eugene Mozgalevsky

Book Manager
Michelle Lo

Production Manager
David Joinnides

President and Publisher,
Sixth&Spring Books
Art Joinnides

Library of Congress Cataloging-in-Publication Data

Mullaney, Colleen, 1966-
Faux fabulous florals: four seasons of easy ideas/ [Colleen Mullaney].
p.cm.
ISBN: 1-931543-39-9
1. Flower arrangement. 2. Artificial flowers. I. Title

SB449.3A7M85 2004
745.92 – dc21   2003057295

Manufactured in China

For Mom and Dad,
who have been a constant source
of support and inspiration and
have taught me that following
your dreams is always worth it,
as you never know where
they may lead.

contents

My love of flowers started at an early age. As far back as I can remember, I was enthralled by the changing seasons of the Pennsylvania countryside. Each season offered something new and exciting. I delighted in picking the first daffodils of spring in the nearby woods and watering the brightly colored zinnias in abundant bloom in my parents' summer garden. Every fall, I marveled at the trees ablaze with color and the pumpkins everywhere; the sight and smell of fresh pine boughs adorned with bright red berries and shiny ribbons always meant winter and the holidays to me. The colors, shapes and scents of the different seasons always amazed me. By the time I was a teenager, I was planting masses of flowers for cutting each spring and summer, collecting berries and leaves through the fall and decorating the house with fresh evergreens for the Christmas holidays. My arrangements and displays soon became a year-round hobby, as I was always finding inspiration from nature and new ways with flowers.

My hobby remained my passion and became my profession. I continued working with fresh flowers and discovered the versatility and possibilities of dried flowers. As I began designing arrangements for shops and private clients, I spent more time in the flower market and floral supply shops. In the market, I noticed more and more silk flowers (as they were once called—I call them "faux," as they contain really very little or no silk.) They appeared in greater variety and improved quality, and I began experimenting with incorporating them into my arrangements. A career as an editor in the crafting and home decorating fields soon followed, and I found myself increasingly turning to faux materials in the wide assortment of arrangements that I made for magazines and books. It was during that time, when the market was becoming abundant with faux materials, that my appetite for them grew. Now, the possibilities for varied, colorful and interesting faux floral arrangements are endless. I still love working with fresh flowers, but I have come to prefer faux over dried, which tend to fade, turn brittle and shed, losing their appeal over time. Faux floral arrangements always look lovely and need little or no maintenance besides occasional dusting. Through the years and seasons, I have become an avid fan and design enthusiast of faux flowers.

This book will inspire you to discover the joy and satisfaction of working with faux florals and creating arrangements and displays for your home. When you let the seasons be your guide, you will discover colors, interesting textures and a variety of materials for arrangements that celebrate every month of the year. Each project has a materials list and how-to instructions for easy arranging. I hope you will have as much fun creating these arrangements as I had, and I'm quite sure you will come to your own appreciation and newfound, or newly rekindled, love of faux florals.

—Colleen Mullaney

about faux florals

Not only has the assortment and variety greatly improved but so have the color spectrum and quality. At times it is even difficult to tell fresh from faux. The enthusiasm of arrangers and crafters combined with the desire to have flowers in the home year-round have led manufacturers to produce greater varieties of faux flowers, with higher quality and detail. The expanded palette is virtually limitless, ranging from a vivid red gerbera to the palest pink tulip. Encouragement from designers and floral enthusiasts worldwide has led the industry to expand its inventory, which now encompasses fruits, vegetables, berries, nuts and more unusual plants, from the exotic to herbs and wildflowers.

Most high-quality faux flowers available today are produced in Asia, where they are designed with exceptional botanical accuracy. Shaped from sculpted molds, they are superior in every way to the earlier fabric flowers. Although still referred to as silk, they are crafted from synthetic fibers. The fabric is pressed over heated molds that melt the plastic fibers and form the shape and character of a particular flower, producing the cupped petals of tulips or the blousy bloom of a peony. First, details are painted on and wire stems are covered, then the flowers are assembled piece by piece. Finally, they are carefully packed, to protect them during the long shipping process.

When choosing faux flowers, look for ones that have a lifelike appearance. If you want to bend over and smell them, you know it's a high-quality faux. Often in the shops, other consumers will watch in disbelief as I sniff the flowers. I can almost smell the perfume of the garden rose or the intoxicating scent of a handful of sweet peas.

■ Avoid flowers that appear shiny and waxy, as they will certainly continue to appear that way in an arrangement. Look at the leaves. Do they seem real? Is the foliage veined and lifelike? Do the poppy petals resemble layers of paper, and are they shaped like buttercups? Choose flowers in which the colors match their natural counterpart. For instance, neon-blue cosmos would never look real. Pay particular attention to the flowers' details—the most impor-tant element in choosing faux flowers.

■ Take care not to damage the stems and foliage of faux florals. The stems of such flowers as ranunculi and sunflowers have a soft, fuzzy coating that imitates their real counterparts; when removing the tags or foliage from the stems, do it carefully so as not to scratch or remove this coating.

■ Some faux flowers are particularly pli-able and easy to work with. Roses, for instance, can be easily pried open to resemble a full bloom or, if individual petals are wired, they can be unfolded and manipulated into any shape desired. This is one of the best advantages of working with faux flowers. Look for flowers with wired stems, as they will be easier to work with—you can bend them to fit any style of arrangement or display and any kind of container.

*H*aving the necessary tools on hand allows you to concentrate on the project. If you do a lot of arranging, you should have a toolbox or prop-kit, to which you can add over time. The wide variety of materials available to crafters and floral enthusiasts grows ever wider as new and innovative tools and supplies show up on the market every year.

One of the most important tools is a sharp pair of wire cutters. I've found it to be the key to arranging faux flowers, and have tried substitutes with limited success. A good heavy-duty pair runs between $20 and $30. If you can't find a decent pair in a crafts store, try a hardware store or home-improvement warehouse.

Use smaller scissors to cut materials such as leaves, petals and ribbons. Do keep the scissors sharp, as these details are very important to achieving a finished look for your arrangement.

Use a sharp knife for shaping and trimming the foam blocks that fit into containers and vases. I use an old kitchen knife with a long, wide blade, and it works perfectly.

Glue guns are great tools for affixing mosses and foam to containers, as well as securing large faux items such as fruits and vegetables. They are available in both low- and high-heat varieties, and there are even adjustable ones. I used to be a huge fan of them, hot-gluing everything, but I have burned my fingers more than enough over the years and now rely on clear tacky adhesive whenever I can, using my glue gun only where best suited.

Floral wires and tapes are also essentials for arranging. Wires come in different gauges. Medium gauge is suitable for most stems. For delicate leaves and blossoms, I use thinner wire. Wire is a basic for crafting wreaths but also the key to extending the length of flowers where stems may be a bit short.

Floral tapes come in rolls, in shades of

green and brown. I use dark green, as it resembles the stems' natural color and will blend easily into an arrangement. The rolls are self-sealing and are activated by the heat in your fingers once the tape is pulled apart. They can be used for securing a block of foam to a container or for binding stems together. Double-sided tape is useful, as it is sticky on both sides, for adhering materials like bamboo and twigs to containers or sides of votives or vases. Double-sided clear tape is also wonderful for wrapping gifts, as the result is a clean-cornered wrap job and a much better presentation.

Pins are often used to attach clumps of green moss to a foam base or a ribbon to a wreath. U-pins will hold these materials in place and are much easier than devising a wire holder. T-pins are used in the same way, but for smaller jobs, like attaching ribbons, raffia strands and leaves.

Quick Water™ solution or a resin kit creates the illusion of fresh water. I love working with this relatively new product because it makes the faux flowers seem so real. Be sure to follow all of the manufacturers' instructions when using these products.

bases

*T*hese are the foundation pieces from which the arrangement is made. Floral foam, designed for faux arrangements, comes in many different shapes and sizes. The most common shape is the brick, (or rectangular) shape, but also available in cones, rings, balls and boards. Boards, which can be cut into any length or width desired, are particularly useful when making a tablescape, a design that runs the length of the table. Today, topiary forms are often prefabricated, with woodlike stems. They come in a variety of sizes, for easy arranging.

If you want to add candles to the arrangement, plastic candleholders are extremely helpful, available in taper or pillar form; they come with legs that secure them into the foam. Insert the holder where the candle will be and make your arrangement around it.

With the faux market taking off, there are more and more interesting materials to work with. Ribbons come in any pattern, color and width, complementing arrangements by adding a dash of color or contrast. Raffia is available in a rainbow of colors. Ropes and twines come in several colors, textures and degrees of thickness. Faux fruits, vegetables, eggs and berries are made with fine, natural elements. Mosses are available in deep shades of green, mimicking the natural color of stems and providing better camouflage of the floral foam or clay in arrangements. Polished rocks, shells and colored glass are all fun to work with and can add texture and interest to displays. So when you are collecting shells, beach glass, or pretty pebbles remember that they might be useful for future arrangements.

spring

*T*he vibrant colors
of spring—bright tulips,
graceful irises and bushels of
daffodils—wake us up after a long,
cold winter. It's the perfect time to
create some of these arrangements
for your home, filling it with
the spirit of the season.

spring's faux blooms

CLOCKWISE FROM LEFT: purple
sweet pea, clark rose
ranunculus, daffodil, pink
peony, tulip, cream viburnums,
dark purple ranunculus,
bleeding heart.

daffodil days

White narcissi and lime-green mop-heads of viburnum accent the soft yellow shades of daffodils. Set this arrangement in a classic container, and it adds a touch of spring to any room.

materials

10 stems yellow daffodils

6 stems white narcissi

5 stems green viburnums

decorative urn

floral foam

hot-glue gun and glue sticks

how to

1. Fill urn with floral foam, glue in place.
2. Cut stems of daffodils and arrange as shown; cut and arrange narcissi and viburnums.
3. Bend stems to create a cascading effect.

NOTE: If heads of viburnums are too floppy, simply wire the stems with floral wire before arranging in container.

pot luck

*P*retty pots adorn this festive table with springtime flair. Topiaries fashioned from bright and fluffy orange- and rose-colored ranunculi have a garden-fresh look. Add extra whimsy to the setting with "place-card eggs" and small saucers filled with moss.

materials

7 stems each, rose and orange ranunculi

1 stem curly willow

2 decorative 4" (10cm) pots

floral foam

green moss

green string

hot-glue gun and glue sticks

FOR PLACE-CARD EGGS:

4" (10cm) terracotta saucers

green moss

faux eggs

gold marker

to make topiaries

1. Gather seven stems of same-color ranunculi in a tight bunch and tie together with string just under blossoms' heads. Carefully remove all foliage from stems.
2. Cut foam to fit in pots, glue to secure.
3. Holding bunch of ranunculus, press bottom of stems into the center of foam. Press firmly, as this will create the topiary stem.
4. Cut willow into several wispy pieces, press into foam next to floral stems and wrap willow around ranunculus stems in a whimsical pattern.
5. Cover foam with moss, glue down, trimming any excess.

to make place-cards

1. Fill each saucer with moss, glue to secure.
2. Using gold marker, write each person's name on side of eggs. Let marker dry.
3. Place eggs in center of each mound of moss.

rhapsody in blue

ydrangeas and clusters of sweet peas in deep blues and purples, coupled with rich-yellow daffodils, make this arrangement sing spring. This candle-ring looks great as a centerpiece indoors or out. For an alternative, omit the candle and glass hurricane and hang on a door or wall.

materials

12 stems daffodils

4 stems purple hydrangeas

6 stems purple sweet peas

6 stems light-blue sweet peas

2 blossoms lilac

3 bunches green-grape clusters

12" (30cm) foam ring

floral wire

6" (15cm) white pillar candle

glass hurricane

to make ring

1. Using green floral wire, secure one hydrangea blossom to foam ring. Working in a circular pattern, wire on bunch of three daffodils, followed by three purple sweet peas, lilac blossom, and a cluster of grapes. Repeat this pattern, starting with hydrangea blossom and alternating colors of sweet peas until ring is covered.

2. Place candle in hurricane and position in ring.

peonies on parade

Peonies are the official symbol of spring in China, their birthplace. Although these powder-puff blossoms can be found in fresh-flower markets in many colors, from deep crimson to pale pink to soft yellow, it is only in the last few years that these shades have become available in faux flowers. The peonies' large heads are perfect for arranging en masse, and their fluffy petals overlap to hide floral foam. Faux peonies are available in both the single- and double-flowering varieties, but for arrangements I prefer the sensational and showy blooms of the doubles.

Here, the blue and white ceramic vase accents the vibrant peony mix; the oval shape is ideal for showcasing the blousy blooms. Just a few buds and sprigs of foliage add dashes of color and interest to this timeless display.

materials

peony stems: 10 deep pink, 5 raspberry, 5 creamy white-with pink accent
ceramic container
floral foam
clear tacky adhesive

how to

1. Fill the container with floral foam and secure with adhesive.
2. Cut the peony stems to desired lengths, place in vase, bending the stems to show the face of the flower and soften the look.
3. Finish by filling in with buds and foliage.

tip

For casual flair, try filling an old coffee can or a pitcher with these beautiful blooms.

full bloom

*T*his rustic, weathered wooden box works well with such an opulent display of flowers. Ruffled parrot tulips with bright orange and yellow stripes announce spring is officially here. The combination of vibrant tones is sure to awaken the senses after the winter months!

materials

7 stems parrot tulips

6 stems deep-purple ranunculi

4 stems pink variegated tulips

6 snowball viburnum blossoms

1 branch pink apple blossoms

6 stems daffodils

wooden box

floral foam

hot glue gun and glue sticks

floral wire

how to

1. Fill box with floral foam, glue to secure.
2. Cut stems and arrange as shown, grouping types of flowers together when possible for maximum visual impact.
3. Fashion "ribbons" at the base of the arrangement by bending tulip foliage in half and securing ends in floral foam with wire.

sweet seat

Rich-purple bearded irises add a lovely accent when wrapped in an antique handkerchief tied with a gingham bow. Use a wire-edged ribbon in lavender or blue to attach this posy to a chair.

idea

For assigned seating, add a 12″ (30cm) strip of satin ribbon printed with each guest's name and fasten around handkerchief with a gingham ribbon to create a double bow. Guests can take this home as a personalized gift.

materials

2 bearded irises in purple tones

small square white handkerchief

12″ (30cm) purple and white gingham ribbon, $5/8$″ (15mm) wide

18″ (46cm) lavender wire-edged ribbon, $1\frac{1}{2}$″ (39mm) wide

floral wire

how to

1. Cut iris stems to 4″ (10cm) in length. Wire together.
2. Wrap stems in handkerchief. Secure with gingham ribbon and tie bow to finish.
3. To hang, loop wire-edged ribbon over top of chair and tie ends together under irises.

welcome ring

A simple bouquet tied on a grapevine base makes a sweet adornment for a guest-room door. Gather a sampling of spring blossoms such as tulip, ranunculus, sweet pea and bleeding heart. Attach the bouquet to a small grapevine wreath with floral wire; finish by adding pink and green ribbon for a bright accent of color.

materials

6″ (15cm) grapevine wreath

1 stem each pink tulip, light pink rannuculus, pink sweet pea, lavender bleeding heart

24″ (60cm) each pink and green grosgrain ribbon, ⅞″ (23mm) wide

floral wire

how to

① Cut stems and form small bouquet.

② Wire to secure bouquet, then wire bouquet onto grapevine wreath.

③ Wrap ribbons around wreath, forming loop at top, knot to secure.

country charm

*P*eonies are a classic wedding flower; this basket, filled with soft pink and white blooms, suits a bridesmaid, flower girl or garden reception. A faux arrangement creates an instant keepsake of the special day. Ribbon loops of pink and white gingham-check sweetly offset the soft, powdery blooms.

materials

3 stems pink peonies

3 stems cream-with-pink-accent peonies

floral foam

clear tacky adhesive

18" (45cm) small gingham check ribbon for loops, $5/8$" (15mm) wide

12" (30cm) gingham check ribbon for hanging, $7/8$" (23mm) wide

decorative basket

how to

1. Fill the basket with floral foam, glue to secure.
2. Cut the peony stems and arrange as shown.
3. To make loops, cut ribbon into 6" (15cm) lengths, wire ends together.
4. Insert wires into foam.
5. Hang basket.

high-wire act

$\mathscr{C}$ontainers can add a lot of personality to arrangements, making them formal, casual, modern or whimsical. I found this rustic wire-holder complete with glass vase in a small gift shop and thought it would be perfect for a posy. Set simple stems of lilac, peony and rose tied with a jewel-toned sheer ribbon in a vase of Quick Water™. Hang from a shelf or mantle for a decorative room accent.

materials

1 stem each lilac, pink peony, peach rose
decorative wire container with glass vase
12″ (30cm) sheer purple ribbon, 1″ (25mm) wide
Quick Water™ solution
floral wire

how to

1. Cut stems and form small cluster. Secure with floral wire.
2. Fill vase two-thirds full with Quick Water™ solution. Arrange flowers in vase and let set according to manufacturer's instructions.
3. When set, tie ribbon around stems and form bow.
4. Set vase in wire container and hang.

sweet water

*F*lowers in soft, pastel shades give this arrangement a vintage look. A watering can in an antiqued shade of off-white makes for a complementary container. Offset tulips, blush-toned ranunculi and lime-green berries with lavender scabiosas; a strategically placed rose ranunculus adds a dash of color. Other ideal containers would be old sap buckets, weathered garden pots or antique flower buckets.

materials

6 peach ranunculi

5 lavender scabiosas

4 light pink tulips

5 white tulips

1 stem lime-green berries

2 rose ranunculi

floral foam

clear tacky adhesive

watering can

how to

1. Fill watering can with floral foam. Glue to secure.
2. Cut stems and arrange as shown.

pretty packages

It's lovely to see a person's face light up when he is presented with a beautifully wrapped gift. Although he might be thinking that a lot of time and energy went into the preparations, it is actually simple and quick to turn an ordinary gift into something extra special.

take-out time
Packaging stores now carry these fast-food containers. This one has a sprig of lilac festively attached to the side, with coordinated purple polka-dotted tissue completing the look.

branching out
A sprig of dogwood and a fluffy viburnum is a perfect addition to spring's pale-green palate. Simply tie on the faux stems with the bow.

terrific toppers
Think outside the box and go with a can! Grosgrain ribbons in matching colors dress up a simple aluminum canister. For added flair, top them off with a blousy peony or an assortment of sweet pea blossoms.

materials
decorative ribbons
1 stem cream peony
aluminum can
clear tacky adhesive

how to
1. Measure the circumference of the can and cut ribbons to this measurement, plus 1″ (2.5cm).
2. Starting at the bottom, glue ribbons to can; overlap ends slightly. Continue working from bottom to top, overlapping ribbons to ensure can is completely covered.
3. Cut peony stem to just under the flower. Glue on top of can. Let dry. Fill can with gift.

sweet glow

Nothing says spring quite like a bunch of sweet peas, with their ruffled petals and butterfly-shaped flowers. Sweet peas are now available in a rainbow of colors at craft and floral supply stores. This easy-to-make candle-ring is fashioned in purple and pink shades, but substitute your favorite colors or choose colors that fit your decorating scheme and complement your home.

materials

30 stems sweet peas: 10 purple, 10 lavender, 10 pink
terracotta pot
floral foam
8" (20cm) candle
plastic candleholder
clear tacky adhesive

how to

1. Cut foam to fit pot and glue to secure.
2. Place candleholder in center of foam and press in.
3. Cut the sweet pea stems to desired length and, working in a clockwise direction, insert stems in foam. Stems should be long enough to bend over the edge of the pot covering, about one-third down the side of the pot.
4. Cut some stems shorter to fill in around the candleholder and the center of arrangement.
5. Continue until foam is covered with the sweet pea flowers. Cut and use any leftover tendrils, unwinding them for added effect.
6. Add candle.

branches in bloom

*B*looming branches are one of the first signs spring is upon us. Why not create a beautiful ring of colorful blooms? Hang on a door, window or front porch to welcome the season's first show of color.

materials

6 stems assorted spring blossoms, including dogwood, cherry and apple

1 stem bleeding heart

3 faux eggs

gold acrylic craft paint

Spanish moss

14" (35cm) grapevine wreath

1 yard (.9m) decorative ribbon, 1½" (39mm) wide

hot glue gun and glue sticks

small piece of sponge

how to

1. Cut stems to 4" (10cm) in length.
2. Starting on left side of wreath, wire on bunches of branches, working down to bottom.
3. Starting on the right side, wire on bunches of branches, working down towards the bottom, leaving a small gap to place eggs.
4. Glue Spanish moss in gap between branches, creating a small nest for eggs.
5. Use sponge to dab eggs with paint to achieve a mottled look. When dry, glue eggs to nest of Spanish moss.

summer

Glorious colors
in vibrant shades are found among
summer's bounty. To bring the season indoors,
use masses of brightly colored flowers in displays,
or just a few for a spot of color here and there.
Cool down summer's intense hues by either
adding white to the arrangement or
such elements as green foliage,
shells or candles.

zinnias in a basket

*M*ix simple pleasures with summertime fun with this patriotic display. Playfully arrange bright red zinnias in small glass jars nestled in wicker; the flowers are perfect for outdoor parties and easy to arrange.

materials

3 stems red zinnias

glass jars and wicker-basket set

Quick Water™ solution

how to

1. Fill jars two-thirds full with Quick Water™ solution.
2. Arrange zinnias and let set according to manufacturer's instructions.
3. Place jars in wicker holder

tip

For more patriotic flair, add a small flag or two to each jar.

into the woods

Soft green faux ferns glued to a frosted votive have nature's touch. Frost your own votive holders with sprays and kits available from craft stores.

materials

6 green fern leaves
frosted votive
votive candle
clear tacky adhesive

how to

① **Glue ferns onto frosted votive, let dry.**
② **Place candle in votive and light.**

petal power

Bright purple delphinium blossoms bedeck this clear-glass votive. These are a perfect table-topper for dining alfresco in the warm summer months. Gorgeous when made with delphinium blossoms of different shades or any flower with medium-sized blooms. For my brother's wedding dinner, I made thirty from purple and blue delphiniums. As centerpieces and scattered about, the effect was magical. My mother still uses them for entertaining outdoors.

materials for one votive

3 stems purple delphiniums

glass votive

small pillar candle

clear tacky adhesive

how to

1. Cut blossoms from stems. Be sure to cut close enough that the base is flat.

2. Starting at the bottom of the votive and working in a circular pattern, glue on blossoms. Make sure they are all similar in size and shape, creating a uniform look.

3. Let dry.

rosy glow

*S*et in a beautiful rose blossom, these votives make perfect garden-party lights. Line a walkway, or set a bunch down on the table for a truly blooming centerpiece. Scatter extra petals amongst the votives for added appeal.

materials for one votive

1 large pink rose

glass votive

votive candle in coordinating color

clear tacky adhesive

how to

1. Cut rose blossom from stem so that the bloom sits flat.
2. Cut out center bud and a few surrounding petals, leaving enough space for glass votive.
3. Glue glass to center of blossom, let dry.
4. Add candle.
5. Scatter petals as desired.

tiki lights

These night lights are very easy to make and look fantastic when lit. One advantage of faux reed stems is that it doesn't crack when cut or lose its beautiful green color over time.

materials

6 reed stems (equisetum)
glass votive
votive candle
clear tacky adhesive

how to

1. Remove wire supports from reed stems by slicing up side with a sharp knife to expose wire.
2. Measure votive height and cut stalks to appropriate length. If stalks get thinner at the top, use only the wider, bottom pieces, so all of the stalks will be uniform in size.
3. Glue around votive, starting in one place and working around until votive is covered.
4. Let dry.

NOTE: Reed stems may be labelled or sold as bamboo at your local craft store.

party dress

*J*azz up a plain glass votive and add instant party spirit. This festive raffia can be found in craft and floral supply stores in a rainbow of colors; you can make any combination that will suit your party theme or outdoor décor.

materials

raffia in bright pink, orange and purple

glass votive

votive candle

hot-glue gun and glue sticks

how to

1. Measure circumference of votive. Cut raffia to this measurement plus 1″ (2.5cm). Cut twenty strands of each color.

2. Make a bunch for each color and knot the ends of each bunch. There should be three bunches in all—one for each color.

3. Glue knotted end of first bunch to top of glass, let dry.

4. Wrap this first bunch around glass, keeping raffia taut, glue other knotted end to glass, overlapping first knot slightly.

5. Let dry.

6. Continue with bunches of other colors until votive is covered.

making waves

Long walks on the beach can provide a treasure trove of shells, beach glass and driftwood that can add interest to any ocean-inspired arrangement. Most craft and floral supply stores carry these items, but adding your own mementos from holiday trips is a sure conversation-starter. A crisp white bucket makes the perfect container for masses of blue hydrangeas. Today, candles are available in almost any color and shape. I found this candle, with its sea-inspired color and unusual square shape, and thought it would be a great match for the bucket of summer hydrangeas.

materials

4 stems blue hydrangeas
1 starfish
Spanish moss
white bucket
floral foam
decorative candle
hot-glue gun and glue sticks
plastic candleholder

how to

1. Fill bucket with floral foam, glue to bottom. Press candleholder into center of foam.
2. Cut hydrangea heads into smaller blossoms.
3. Starting at the front and working in a circular motion around the candleholder, fill in with hydrangea blossoms. Be sure the top rim of the bucket is completely covered with blossoms.
4. Glue starfish to small patch of moss, glue moss and starfish to hydrangea blooms.
5. Place candle in holder.

beach comber

*T*his arrangement is lovely as the centerpiece of a buffet table or mantel. White hydrangeas, accented with shells, beach glass and rope and topped off by a marine-blue candle, give this arrangement its dockside appeal.

materials

5 stems white hydrangeas

1 large starfish

assortment of shells

assortment of beach glass

30" (75cm) rope—longer if tying napkins

pillar candle

Spanish moss

16" x 1" x 6" (40cm x 2.5cm x 15cm) piece of Styrofoam

u-pins

hot-glue gun and glue sticks

how to

1. Glue layer of moss on top and sides of Styrofoam base. Let dry.
2. Mark placement for candle and remove.
3. Cut hydrangea heads into smaller clusters and glue to foam base until it's covered.
4. Glue starfish to cluster of hydrangeas, tucking part of the starfish underneath blossoms, as shown.
5. Glue one scallop shell inside-up so that sea glass can be layered to this surface.
6. Glue remaining shells outside-up.
7. Wrap rope around shells and along the hydrangea in a pleasing pattern and secure to Styrofoam with u-pins.
8. Glue candle down on marked spot. Let dry.

tip

Driftwood collected at the beach makes a nice sea-swept base for this arrangement.

rose parade

A charming cupful of summer roses in bloom makes an ideal bedside bouquet. The celadon-green shades of the variegated ivy, along with the floppy viburnums and unripe blueberries, are a perfect match for the raspberry- and lilac-colored garden roses.

materials

6 stems lavender roses

3 stems raspberry roses

3 small viburnum heads

4 sprigs green blueberries, or other small green berry

2 sprigs variegated ivy

floral foam

silver cup

clear tacky adhesive

how to

1. Cut foam and fill silver cup, glue to bottom.
2. Cut lavender rose stems and arrange across top, as shown.
3. Cut raspberry roses and fill in.
4. Add viburnum, berries and ivy.
5. For a natural look, be sure the ivy is trailing. The asymmetrical appearance of the arrangement adds to its fresh-from-the-garden look.

peachy intentions

*R*oses and berries are a true summertime combination. The antiqued iron urn enhances the softness of the garden roses as they drape and spill over. The berry foliage adds the finishing touch of carefree grace. Try this arrangement on a porch or patio.

materials

8 peach garden roses

4 pink garden roses

6 deep pink small old-fashioned garden roses with yellow centers

1 stem raspberries with multiple sprigs

floral foam

antiqued urn

clear tacky adhesive

how to

1. Fill urn with foam, glue to bottom.
2. Starting with peach roses, cut stems and arrange in foam, as shown; continue with pink garden roses and then the pink roses with yellow centers.
3. Bend stems over edges and fluff petals where necessary.
4. Fill in with sprigs of raspberry fruit and foliage.

fiesta time

*S*triking arrangements can be fashioned from almost anything, like these paper lanterns filled with vibrant gerberas in coordinating colors. They make a real statement and create an instant party atmosphere!

materials

7 stems each, magenta, orange, and yellow gerberas

paper lanterns in same colors as flowers (Lanterns, which come in a variety of sizes, are available in party supply stores.)

floral wire

how to

1. Make three bouquets, one of each color.
2. Wrap ends with floral wire.
3. Place into lanterns.

garden variety

*T*here's nothing quite like a summer bouquet from the garden. The best part about this one is that it will last all season long. The key to this bouquet is the variety of flowers and the casual way it's fashioned together. Finish it off with a pretty striped ribbon. It makes a delightful hostess gift or centerpiece when dining al fresco.

materials

3 stems sunflowers

2 stems each, pink and purple larkspurs

2 stems blue snapdragons

2 stems yellow freesias

3 stems purple salvias

2 stems orange zinnias

2 stems purple phloxes

24" (60cm) decorative ribbon, 1½" (39mm) wide

how to

1. Remove excess foliage from flower stems.

2. Gather three sunflowers, one phlox and one larkspur, and make small bunch.

3. To this initial bunch, add flowers of your choosing, working around the original bouquet in a clockwise direction until all the flowers are used and a nice round bouquet is formed.

4. Cut stems to about 14" (35cm) in length.

5. Holding the bouquet just under the flower heads, wrap floral wire around stems to secure.

6. Add decorative ribbon and tie a bow.

vine-ripe

nspired by the topiary's recent popularity, I came up with the idea of using little cherry tomatoes in a standard arrangement. The variety of faux fruits and vegetables available today is abundant; in fact, I found these faux tomatoes at a very popular home-supply store. Set this adorable trio on the table, and you'll have people trying to pick the fruits right off!!

materials

40 cherry tomatoes

1 large green cabbage

12″ (30cm) topiary form

6″ (15cm) clay pot and saucer

green moss

raffia

hot-glue gun and glue sticks

how to

1. Cut bottom of topiary form to fit pot, glue to secure. Cover foam at top of pot with moss, glue in place. Start gluing tomatoes to form, placing them close together, alternating with top and bottoms showing. Continue until form is completely covered.

2. Using the points of a pair of scissors, fill in small gaps between tomatoes with moss. Glue in place.

3. Cut large cabbage leaves and place on sides of pot, trims bottoms of leaves so tops just graze rim of clay pot, fold bottoms under pot, glue leaves in place.

4. To finish, wrap several strands of raffia around pot and tie knot.

to make votives

1. Cut smaller leaves from cabbage head.

2. Wrap around votive, trimming bottoms so that tops of leaves graze rims of votives. Fold bottoms under votive and glue in place.

3. To finish, wrap several strands of raffia around votive and tie knot.

tip

Other possible fruits and vegetables for the topiary (all with the same round shape) are lemons, limes, small peaches and apples, or any large berry.

buttoned up

An informal arrangement such as these zinnias wrapped in blue-and-white checked fabric is perfect for a children's party or other casual affair. I made one with pink-and-white checked fabric for my daughter's room and she keeps it on her nightstand year-round. Rickrack trimmed with buttons adds the perfect touch of whimsy.

materials

8 stems medium pink zinnias

8 stems deep pink zinnias

8" (20cm) clear glass vase with scalloped edge

Quick Water™ solution

14" (35cm) square piece of blue-and-white checked fabric

24" (60cm) length of white rickrack

4 buttons, 2 deep pink, 2 light pink

clear tacky adhesive

how to

1. Prepare Quick Water™ solution and fill vase two-thirds full.

2. Cut zinnias to desired length and arrange in vase. Zinnias should be uniform in height, to create a mound effect.

3. Let solution set according to manufacturer's instructions.

4. Place vase in center of fabric, glue bottom of vase to fabric and work around the vase, bringing the fabric up and tucking it into the mouth of the vase until vase is covered.

5. Wrap the rickrack around the vase just under the lip; tie to secure.

6. Glue the two smaller light-pink buttons into the deep-pink ones; glue each set onto ends of rickrack. Let dry.

tip

A simple vase can be dressed up with any kind of fabric, from silk and velvet for formal holiday looks to denims, ticking, or eyelets for country-casual appeal.

roman holiday

*R*eminiscent of al fresco dinners in the Italian countryside, this rustic centerpiece with votives works perfectly for warm summer evenings outdoors. I use these for an informal wine-and-cheese gathering of neighbors. When the centerpiece is paired with small bowls of fresh olives, my guests think it's fresh!

materials

5 olive branches

5 stems lemon leaves

floral foam

decorative olive pot or other green ceramic container

2 6" (15cm) distressed clay pots

2 votive candles

hot-glue gun and glue sticks

to make the arrangement

1. Fill pot with floral foam, glue to bottom.
2. Cut branches to desired length and arrange in pot, bending several stems to create a natural look, as shown.
3. You may have to fluff out lemon leaves, as they come flat and layered together.

to make votives

1. Cut one olive branch to cover circumference of pot rim.
2. Wrap around rim and twist wired ends of branch to secure, glue in place where ends meet. In a few other spots around rim where a leaf meets the pot, place a dab of glue on the underside and press to adhere.
3. Arrange any leaves that are sticking too far off the pot by bending them around the rim.

daisy days

*T*hese happy flowers are a recognized symbol of summertime and simple times. A baby shower with a daisy theme inspired this topiary. I thought it would be a perfect centerpiece and a wonderful keepsake for the baby's nursery. It was a big hit and very simple to make.

materials

10 stems white daisies, or approximately 70 blossoms

two-tiered topiary form

4 yards (3.66m) yellow-and-white checked ribbon, ½" (1.3cm) wide

white pot

green moss

clear tacky adhesive

u-pins

floral wire

how to

1. Glue base of form to bottom of pot.
2. Cut all but four daisies from stems. Starting at the top of one tier, glue daisies to form. Place them close together so that the petals overlap, creating a full look. Continue until both tiers of the topiary are completely covered with daisies.
3. Using a u-pin, attach one end of checked ribbon to the underside of the top ball, right where the stem meets the ball. Begin wrapping the ribbon around the stem in a diagonal pattern. Wrap stem between top and bottom ball, cut and, with another u-pin, attach ribbon to top of bottom ball.
4. Repeat for the stem between bottom ball and base.
5. Fill in top of pot with moss, and glue in place.
6. Make a small bouquet from remaining daisies and a bow from remaining ribbon, wire together and attach to moss with a u-pin.

indian summer

like this arrangement as it is a perfect transition from late summer into early fall. The first autumnal touch of berries, bittersweet and viburnums are mixed with the garden's last hurrah of fiery reds and burnt oranges. The green ceramic pitcher plays off the streaked dahlias, golden sunflowers and cherry tomato stems.

materials
4 stems large orange and yellow dahlias
6 stems yellow marigolds
3 stems golden sunflowers
3 stems orange zinnias
2 stems yellow black-eyed Susans
1 stem cherry tomatoes
floral foam
ceramic pitcher
clear tacky adhesive

how to
1. Fill pitcher with foam and glue to bottom.
2. Cut dahlias, marigolds and other flowers to desired length. Arrange in pitcher, starting with the largest flowers (dahlias and sunflowers) and filling in with the smaller ones.
3. Insert a length of the tomato vine on either side of the pitcher for a draping effect.

farm-stand fresh

*C*apture the best of the season with this adorable arrangement of fruits. Plump peaches surround cherries and clusters of blueberries, all set in a market basket. It's perfect for the kitchen counter or table for a whole season.

materials

4 peaches

15 cherries with stems attached

2 stems blueberries

floral foam

market basket

hot-glue gun and glue sticks

green moss

how to

1. Remove clusters of berries from stems.
2. Fill basket with floral foam and glue to bottom. Cover top of foam with moss, glue in place.
3. Place four peaches on the moss in a diamond shape and glue down.
4. On sides and in between peaches, glue clusters of cherries. In any remaining spaces, affix clusters of blueberries, allowing some to cover top of basket rim to create a spilling over effect.

tip

When choosing faux fruit and vegetables at craft and floral supply stores, avoid those that are too shiny, as they will appear fake. Choose fruits that have the most natural coloring, like these peaches, which are as variegated in color as they would be in nature. If the fruits have stems, make sure they also look real—close to their natural counterpart and not too shiny. Finally, if you use fruits and vegetables with fuzzy skins, handle them carefully, as the coating easily comes off with hot glue, craft glues or anything else with adhesive.

monet's garden

The quality of faux sunflowers has improved a great deal lately. The sunflowers are now golden yellow, and the centers are a deeper shade and more distinct in their honeycombed patterns. This is good news, considering that sunflowers are such a big part of the summer season. Also available in the faux markets now are more sophisticated colors: velvety browns, crimsons and russets. Here, the sunflowers' smiling faces, paired with blue hydrangeas, yellow marigolds and orange freesias, resemble an impressionist painting. The weave of the basket adds rustic texture and plays off the chocolate-brown centers of the sunflowers.

materials

5 stems yellow sunflowers, medium-size

6 stems blue hydrangeas

4 stems yellow marigolds

6 stems orange freesias

3 stems blue larkspurs

floral foam

basket

clear tacky adhesive

how to

1. Cut foam to fit basket, and glue to bottom.
2. Cut hydrangea stems and place in foam.
3. Cut sunflowers and place in arrangement, bending the stems so they face outward.
4. Cut marigold, freesia, and larkspur stems and place in arrangement.

autumn

*T*he season's colorful fruits
and berries, bright leaves and highly
textured flowers all command attention and
are perfect ingredients for your home's faux displays.

Texture is the prominent feature in fall arrangements.
Used alone or in combinations, here are some of
the elements that will contribute to displays
you can enjoy year after year… or long
after the pumpkins are gone: branches,
vines, berries, greenery, nuts, fruits,
vegetables, pinecones, pods,
leaves, wildflowers.

autumn accents

CLOCKWISE FROM TOP: maple leaves, grape leaves, pumpkin, gourd, green berries, viburnum berries, red cockscomb, cream peegee hydrangea, orange mum, apple, pale yellow spider mum, sunflower, crab apples, olives.

fall favorite

*T*he great thing about autumn is that you can mix elements more successfully than in any other season. They just seem to go together, with leaves in different shapes and colors marrying perfectly all kinds of different vines and berries. For example, sunflowers look natural next to crab apples, as if nature intended it this way. The masses of autumnal foliage and flowers surrounding the cranberry pillars are set perfectly in this wood-bark container.

materials

3 stems each, maple, yellow and orange oak, and grape leaves

8 stems assorted sunflowers

2 stems viburnum berries

2 stems crab apples

1 cluster bittersweet berries

floral foam

woodland basket

cranberry candles, one each 12" (30cm) pillar and 8" (20cm) pillar

2 plastic candle holders

hot-glue gun and glue sticks

how to

1. Assemble materials. Cut floral foam to fit container and glue to bottom. Place plastic candleholders in center of foam, push down.

2. Cut foliage stems to roughly 8" (20cm) in length. Starting around the perimeter, arrange stems and twist leaves and vines to face out, so that they are trailing down the basket. Continue until base is full.

3. Add accent flowers and foliage of oak leaves, sunflowers and berries. Secure candles in holders.

harvest time

For fall, you don't need to rely on flowers, as foliage and other elements offer endless possibilities. Gourds arranged in this terracotta pot set on a bed of leaves will have everyone wondering if you just got back from pumpkin picking.

materials

4 assorted gourds
1 stem leaves in autumnal shades
floral foam
green moss
6" (15cm) square terracotta pot
tacky glue

how to

1. Cut foam and fill pot, glue to bottom.
2. Top foam with moss, glue in place.
3. Glue on leaves in decorative pattern, bending edges to mimic curling leaves and to create volume from the flat leaves.
4. Glue the gourds to the leaves, as shown, turning them on edge to create a natural look.
5. Fill the spaces between gourds with small leaves, tucking them in the spaces. Glue in place.

out on the vine

Smaller displays of autumnal fruits and foliage are easier to make and require less time than larger, more involved arrangements. A bunch of golden pears are perfect mates to clusters of grapes and their vine foliage.

materials

1 stem pears, or 4 fruits

1 stem grape clusters, foliage and tendrils

floral foam

green moss

6" (15cm) oval terracotta pot

clear tacky adhesive

how to

1. Cut foam and fill pot, glue to bottom. Cover top of foam with moss, glue in place.
2. Place pears in desired manner, some on end and/or on sides, glue down.
3. Arrange grape clusters and leaves around and under pears, glue in place.
4. Be sure leaves and grapevines cover top and upper lip of pot.

mum's the word

Mums come in all different forms, from loose spider mums to tight buttons to large fluffy California mums, shown here in a deep russet shade. Mums are both fun and easy to work with. These vibrant flowers are instant fillers, creating mounds of color and texture. Paired with a sampling of the season, crab apples, apples, sunflowers and berries, this collection set in a market basket makes for an eye-catching display.

materials

2 stems russet California mums

3 stems russet sunflowers

1 stem apples

1 stem crab apples

1 stem fall leaves

1 stem viburnum berries

floral foam

8" (20cm) market basket

tacky glue

how to

1. Cut foam and fill basket, glue to bottom.
2. Cut stems of materials to approximately 9" (23cm) in length.
3. Arrange mums and sunflowers as shown. Fill in with foliage and berries. Add apples and crab apples, filling in any spaces.

berry ring

Something as simple as
this wreath fashioned from clusters
of fruits and berries can be absolutely
breathtaking, and so easy to put together.
Put out a wreath for friends and
neighbors that will welcome
and wow them.

materials

12" (30cm) grapevine wreath

5 stems assorted small fruits and berries

floral wire

how to

1. Cut all fruits and berries into small clusters about 4" (10cm) long.

2. Assemble small mixed groups of fruits and berries, and attach one group at a time to the wreath, working in a clockwise direction and wiring the stems to the wreath. Continue working around ring until fully covered and all fruits and berries have been used.

3. Cut wire and twist around a few pieces of grapevine to finish.

pumpkin picking

*T*his arrangement showcases the obvious and overly large bloom of the dinner-plate dahlia; the pumpkin base brings the autumn indoors.

materials

1 stem orange and yellow dinner-plate dahlia

1 stem fall leaves

1 small pumpkin

1 branch curly willow

floral foam

clear tacky adhesive

small craft saw

how to

1. Mark about 2" (5cm) down from the stem of the pumpkin with a pencil or pen and mark about three or four points around the circumference. Saw top off.

2. In center of the base, cut a hole 2" (5cm) square and about 2" (5cm) deep. Remove all foam beads. Cut piece of floral foam and fill hole, glue to secure.

3. Arrange willow branches in center of foam. Arrange leaves on surface of pumpkin base, so that the cut foam is fully covered. Layer in a pleasing pattern, curling a few and gluing in place. Continue until base is covered.

4. Place dahlia in center of foam, wrap willow branches around dahlia stem. Place pumpkin top at an angle on side of base and glue in place.

berry clear

$\mathcal{A}$ tussie-mussie of autumnal berries makes a simple but elegant statement when arranged in a delicate cut-glass tumbler. Wrapped in golden oak leaves, this collar replaces the usual ribbon, adding a burst of color to the berry cluster. Try different combinations of colored berries and leaves—whatever is available in nearby stores.

materials

3 stems autumnal berries
1 stem yellow oak leaves
decorative tumbler
floral wire
Quick Water™ solution

how to

1. Cut berry clusters and gather into a tight bunch.
2. Border berries with a collar of oak leaves, wrapping leaves around the bunch with the right sides facing outward. Adjust the leaves so that they are symmetrical and even. Wrap tightly and secure with floral wire.
3. Pour Quick Water™ solution in separate container and mix well. Pour into tumbler slowly and fill two-thirds full.
4. Place in a cool dry place to set, following manufacturer's instructions. Carefully place tussie-mussie in glass so it stands straight up.

falling for color

This large arrangement is certainly a showpiece. Mixing the season's elements keeps it visually interesting, while the Tuscan-inspired urn with mustard glazing plays down its size and stature. The arrangement is a versatile piece for today's home. For a formal look, try brass, silver or crystal. Or go casual with a basket, tin container or sap bucket.

materials

3 stems cream peegee hydrangeas

4 stems yellow spider mums

3 stems orange dahlias

4 stems ruby-red cockscombs

2 stems crab apples

3 stems mixed fall foliages

floral foam

urn

clear tacky adhesive

how to

1. Cut foam and fill urn. Glue to bottom.

2. Start with hydrangeas, as they will be the tallest. Place one stem firmly in the foam to the desired height. This will be the tallest point of the arrangement. Fill in with remaining hydrangeas.

3. Arrange flowers in clusters. Begin with the mums and dahlias. Continue filling in with cockscombs, bunches of foliage and crab apples. Add the spider mums last, allowing them plenty of room so their delicate petals are not crushed.

at your place

*W*aste not, want not. Often I take leftover blooms, berries, ribbons, vines and other materials and fashion them into napkin rings. This is a great use of blooms that have broken from their wire stems or of small clusters of berries that were extras. Follow your theme from centerpiece to napkin rings, adding a finishing touch to your affair. These make great gifts as well. Recently, I gave a set of eight orange-mum napkin rings, set on small gold-sprayed grapevine rings as a housewarming gift.

falling leaves
Using a gold glitter pen, write your guests' names on manila tags. Attach a small cluster of leaves together with string. Thread string, with its cluster of leaves, through hole in tag and tie around napkin.

olives
Glue small sprig of olives and leaves to grapevine ring, with the stems facing in one direction. Trim off excess stems and glue to grapevine ring. Place second sprig with stems facing opposite direction, clip stems and glue to secure. With brown grosgrain ribbon, tie center in a decorative knot to hide stems.

berry cluster
Form a small cluster of berries and tie together with floral wire. Tie cluster to grapevine ring with decorative piece of raffia string.

spider mum
Cut flower from wire stem just below head. Glue onto small grapevine ring.

winter

I love using faux flowers year-round but especially over the holidays, when the prices of fresh flowers skyrocket and the flowers often don't last the season. When the weather outside is inclement, the house can be in bloom!

winter floral

FROM LEFT TO RIGHT: burgundy ranunculus, purple anemone, red berries, white phalaenopsis orchid, red holly berry, fuchsia dendrobium orchid, red carnation, oncidium orchid, deep purple ranunculus, variegated ivy.

merry ring

Wreaths are one of my all-time favorites to craft; this eucalyptus wreath was no exception, perfect to welcome family and friends at the front door and announce that the holiday season has begun. It is easy to make and will stand up to brumal weather.

materials

16"(40cm) wire wreath form

12 stems eucalyptus

3 stems red berries

floral wire

how to

1. Cut eucalyptus stems to about 4" (10cm) in length and gather in small bunches.
2. Starting at one point and working in a clockwise direction, wire eucalyptus bunches to the frame. To every third or fourth bunch, add a sprig of red berries. Continue until wreath is covered.
3. Cut wire and twist ends around wreath to finish.

tip

If the country look of red and green is not your style, try spraying the leaves gold or silver for a sparkling holiday, or white for a winter-wonderland effect.

easy elegance

$\mathcal{T}$he carnation has suffered a bad rap in recent years as an old-fashioned, out-of-vogue flower. I have to admit there was a point when I was not their biggest fan. But I have come around and use them in arrangements year-round. Carnations in bright shades of red bedeck this topiary form. Make several and flank both ends of a mantel or table. This no-fuss project will leave you with plenty of time for shopping and holiday activities.

materials

20 stems bright red carnations

20 stems crimson carnations

14″ (35cm) topiary cone

floral foam

decorative urn

clear tacky adhesive

how to

1. Cut floral foam to fill urn, glue to bottom. Glue topiary cone atop foam.
2. Cut carnation stems to 1″ (2.5cm) in length.
3. Starting at the bottom of cone, dab glue on the bottom of stems and press into foam. Work around the base and up the form until completely covered.

gold rush

*T*hese are simple enough to make several for a table centerpiece or kitchen windowsill. The velvety petals of the ranunculus go perfectly with the gilded pots. Frosted berries and wispy ferns add a finishing touch.

materials per pot

4 stems crimson ranunculi

3 stems frosted berries

3 stems plumosus ferns

6" (15cm) gold pot

floral foam

floral wire

how to

① Cut floral foam to fit in pot. Glue to secure.

② Cut ranunculus stems to 8" (20cm) in length and press them into foam so that the stems are approximately 6" (15cm) in length.

③ Surround ranunculus with stems of berries so that you have a layered look.

④ Cut ferns and gather into small bunches, tying ends with wire. Insert wired ends of fern bunches into the foam so that base is covered. Be sure to press down enough so that the wire is hidden from view.

gifts with glam

I've always been a big fan of beautifully presented gifts, but with everyone so short on time these days, that extra touch is harder to come by. These unique and quick packaging ideas will make you feel good— and the recipient fabulous.

purple passion

Cover a can with bright purple orchid blossoms and drop the gift right in. Finish with a plume of lavender tissue and tie with a ribbon. No need for the top here. The blooming container can be used as a pen or makeup-brush holder. Adorning a silver box with velvety anemones and bright limes carries a fresh, modern look into the holiday season.

color on metallic

Spruce up these traditional silvers and golds with orchid sprigs in fuchsia shades. Add ribbons and berries in complementary shades to complete the look.

white wash

A dash of vibrant red and green is all it takes to jazz up winter whites. Red-and-white striped ribbons paired with bright red holly berries adds country charm to the soft white papers. Touches of green evoke nature's way. The package, adorned with a cluster of euphorbia berries and variegated ivy, has a frosty, wintergreen look.

tip

For packages with panache, use elements that share the same color palette.

season sparkler

*T*he benefits of this arrangement are twofold. First, it involves something entirely different from the traditional red and green holiday scheme, bringing a modern edge with the ever-popular silver and jewel-tones. Second, it can be used in your home all winter long, well past the new year. The green limes are a funky element, while the blossoms set in tiny vases make perfect place-cards or decorative details for tablescaping.

materials

9 stems anemones in shades of purple

1 stem limes

silver vase

2 small glass vases

Quick Water™ solution

how to

1. Mix the Quick Water™ solution and fill the vases two-thirds full.

2. Arrange anemones and limes in silver vase and blossoms in smaller vases.

3. Let set over night, following manufacturer's instructions.

hospitality sweet

*A*rrangements for a bedroom should be small and compact. The combination of amaryllises, tulips and ivy does just that. It is simple to put together and will joyfully welcome guests for the holidays. The arrangement would also look lovely either in a bathroom or set on a hall table.

materials

3 stems red amaryllises

3 stems white tulips

3 stems Star of Bethlehems

3 sprigs variegated ivy

floral foam

silver cup

clear tacky adhesive

how to

1. Fill silver cup with foam. Glue to bottom.
2. Cut floral stems short enough so that heads lie just above the rim of the cup, forming a compact dome.
3. Press into foam, starting with the amaryllis stems, then Star of Bethlehems and tulips. Fill in with sprigs of ivy, arranging them so that they trail down the cup.

tip

Cutting the amaryllis can sometimes be difficult, as there may be multiple wires to the stem. Try cutting the stem covering first. Then cut the wires one at a time.

festival of lights

*C*andles are magical and sensuous, and a home comes alive with their soft glow, especially during the holidays and when paired with exotic orchids. The base here is a raised hurricane lamp, but instead of putting the candle inside, I chose to place it on top for greater visual impact.

materials

10 stems white-with-burgandy-accent orchids

hurricane lamp

floral foam

floral tape

green Spanish moss

10" (25cm) burgundy pillar candle

how to

1. Cut foam to fit rim of hurricane. Using floral tape, affix foam to sides of glass. Leaving a space in the center for candle, cover foam with moss, glue in place.

2. Cut and arrange orchid stems so that they fall to cover parts of hurricane. Some should be longer than others for a cascading effect. Bend into shape and twist flowers so that they face outward. Affix base of candle to foam with floral tape.

window dressing

*T*his happy trio set in colored glass vases on a windowsill is a perfect winter's day pick-me-up. I found these glasses in a home-accessories store, where they were actually sold as kitchen jars for oil and vinegar.

materials

3 stems white tulips

3 jewel-toned glass containers

Quick Water™ solution

how to

1. Mix together solution and pour into each container until two-thirds full.
2. Cut tulips and place in containers, bending stems slightly to create a natural look.
3. Let set according to manufacturer's instructions.

shell seeker

Decorative shells such as this one can be found in craft, floral supply, or specialty-shell stores or among your own private collection, of course. I chose this shell for its lovely color and interesting lines, but any good-size shell will do, provided it has ample room for the orchid stem.

materials

1 stem white orchid

1 stem curly willow

decorative shell

floral foam

green moss

clear tacky adhesive

how to

1. Clean and wipe shell.
2. Fill bottom of shell with foam and glue in place.
3. Insert orchid stem in foam, gluing to secure if necessary.
4. Insert willow next to orchid stem and twist around orchid stem so that the two become entwined.

boxed set

*S*leek and modern, this
window box offers a bit of green on
a pale winter day. As alliums have become
increasingly popular with gardeners, they have
also become more readily available in the faux
market. Not easy to work into arrangements,
they look nice standing on their own. This
quartet looks at home in the nesting
boxes. Shiny river rocks atop the
foam make for a natural
finishing touch.

materials

4 stems purple alliums
1 set aluminum nesting boxes
floral foam
river rocks
clear tacky adhesive

how to

1. Cut foam and fill small boxes, gluing to bottoms.
2. Cut alliums to desired length (all four must be the same length). Press stems into foam, checking height and uniformity.
3. Glue river rocks to top of foam, covering it completely.
4. Insert boxes back into tray.

fruited ring

These jeweled fruits set on a bed of lemon leaves make a lovely centerpiece or table accent. I chose a palette of fresh yellows and greens, but there are many other colors available. A simple wreath is the base of this easy-to-make ring; adding a scented candle makes the ring's fruit come to life.

materials

8 pieces jeweled fruit in yellow and green shades

1 package lemon leaves

Spanish moss

8" (20cm) foam wreath with flat bottom

2 yards (1.66m) sheer white wire-edged ribbon, 1½" (39mm) wide

hot-glue gun and glue sticks

floral wire

how to

1. Using floral wire, wrap top of wreath with Spanish moss.
2. Place a layer of lemon leaves around ring, glue to secure.
3. Glue fruit, facing upright, around ring and on top of lemon leaves.
4. Cut ribbon to 4" (10cm) lengths and fold into loops. Gather ends of loops and tie with wire. Add loops of ribbon by inserting the wires into the foam.
5. Add candle.

Jo-Ann Stores Inc.
5555 Darrow Road
Hudson, OH 44236
(330) 656-2600
www.jo-ann.com

Pany Silk Flowers
146 West 28th Street
New York, NY 10001
(212) 645-9526

Planter Resource
106 West 28th Street
New York, NY 10001
(212) 206-7687

Patchogue Floral Fantasyland
10 Robinson Avenue
Patchogue, NY 11772
(631) 475-2059
www.fantasylandonthenet.com

Smith & Hawken
www.SmithandHawken.com

Crate and Barrel
725 Landwehr Road
Northbrook, IL 60062
www.crateandbarrel.com

Pottery Barn
www.potterybarn.com

Container Store
(888) 266-8246
www.containerstore.com

acknowledgments

would like to thank the team who endured brutally long days of photographing with unwavering enthusiasm and support: Jack Deutsch for his beautiful photography and talent; Gene Mozgalevsky, photographer's assistant, for entertaining everyone; and Laura Maffeo, for her stellar propping and styling.

I'd also like to thank Trisha Malcolm, who from day one was a never-ending source of creative support, and for whose friendship I am grateful.

Thank you also to the team at Sixth&Spring Books, especially Michelle Lo, who patiently awaited the photographs and text and managed to get everything in according to schedule.

And last but not least, I'd like to thank my home team, without whose patience and support this book would not have been possible. They have endured buckets of flowers and arrangements everywhere, long days of photography and endless nights of me and my laptop. And so I thank my wonderful husband Jack and our little girl Gracie, who have allowed me to make one of my dreams come true.